Los sentidos

Annabelle Tan

PICTURE CREDITS
Illustration by Shane Nagle (14–15).
Cover, 4 (left), 6 (above right & below right), 7 (right), 12 (left), 13 (left), 16 (bottom), Getty Images; 1, 2, 4 (right), 5 (all), 6 (left), 8 (all), 9 (all), 10, 11 (all), 12 (above right), 16 (above left, above right, center left & center right), Photolibrary.com; 7 (above left), Tony Freeman/PhotoEdit, Inc.; 13 (right), Zefa Images.

Produced through the worldwide resources of the National Geographic Society, John M. Fahey, Jr., President and Chief Executive Officer; Gilbert M. Grosvenor, Chairman of the Board.

PREPARED BY NATIONAL GEOGRAPHIC SCHOOL PUBLISHING
Ericka Markman, Senior Vice President and President Children's Books and Education Publishing Group; Steve Mico, Senior Vice President and Publisher; Marianne Hiland, Editorial Director; Lynnette Brent, Executive Editor; Michael Murphy and Barbara Wood, Senior Editors; Bea Jackson, Design Director; David Dumo, Art Director; Margaret Sidlowsky, Illustrations Director; Matt Wascavage, Manager of Publishing Services; Sean Philpotts, Production Manager.

SPANISH LANGUAGE VERSION PREPARED BY NATIONAL GEOGRAPHIC SCHOOL PUBLISHING GROUP
Sheron Long, CEO; Sam Gesumaria, President; Fran Downey, Vice President and Publisher; Margaret Sidlosky, Director of Design and Illustrations; Paul Osborn, Senior Editor; Sean Philpotts, Project Manager; Lisa Pergolizzi, Production Manager.

MANUFACTURING AND QUALITY MANAGEMENT
Christopher A. Liedel, Chief Financial Officer; George Bounelis, Vice President; Clifton M. Brown III, Director.

BOOK DEVELOPMENT
Ibis for Kids Australia Pty Limited.

SPANISH LANGUAGE TRANSLATION
Tatiana Acosta/Guillermo Gutiérrez

SPANISH LANGUAGE BOOK DEVELOPMENT
Navta Associates, Inc.

Published by the National Geographic Society
Washington, D.C. 20036-4688

Copyright © 2008 National Geographic Society. All rights reserved. Reproduction of the whole or any part of the contents without written permission from the publisher is prohibited. National Geographic, National Geographic School Publishing, National Geographic Windows on Literacy and the Yellow Border are registered trademarks of the National Geographic Society.

ISBN: 978-0-7362-3839-7

Printed in Canada

12 11 10 09 08

10 9 8 7 6 5 4 3 2

Contenido

Pensar y conversar — 4

Ver — 6

Oír — 8

Tocar — 10

Oler — 12

Saborear — 13

Usar lo que aprendieron — 14

Glosario ilustrado — 16

Pensar y conversar

Nuestros sentidos nos permiten ver, oír, tocar, oler y saborear. Digan cómo están usando sus sentidos estos niños.

tocar

saborear

oler

Ver

Podemos **ver** con los **ojos**.

Podemos ver tamaños, colores y formas.

Oír
Podemos **oír** con los **oídos**.

Algunos sonidos son suaves.

Algunos sonidos son fuertes.

Tocar
Podemos **tocar** con las **manos.**

Algunas cosas son ásperas.

Algunas cosas son lisas.

Algunas cosas son calientes.

Algunas cosas son frías.

Oler

Podemos **oler** con la **nariz.**

Algunas cosas huelen mal.

Algunas cosas huelen bien.

Saborear
Podemos **saborear** con la **lengua.**

Algunas cosas son dulces.

Algunas cosas son saladas.

Usar lo que aprendieron

¿Qué podrían ver, oír, tocar, oler y saborear en este lugar?

oír

oler

saborear

sentidos

tocar

ver

Glosario ilustrado

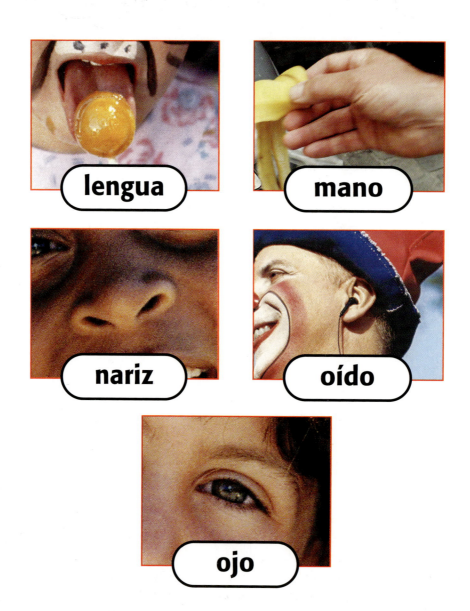